Write It
Publish It
Sell It

The Complete Guide for Aspiring Authors

Write It
Publish It
Sell It

The Complete Guide for Aspiring Authors

By Janelle Villiers

Dedication

Books possess the power to transform lives. My mission is to help you liberate the story within you—to guide your words from thought to publication, empowering you to touch the lives you were destined to change.

To every soul harboring unwritten chapters in their mind and heart: I see your untold story. I honor your silent voice. This book stands as my outstretched hand. Your readers are waiting.

I wrote this book for you ☺

Contents

Introduction: From Dream to Reality

Every author's journey begins with a single thought: *I have something to say.* If you're holding this book, you've likely felt that same spark—a story, a message, or expertise that could inspire, help, or change lives. But perhaps, like so many aspiring authors, you've also faced the doubts, the fear, and the uncertainty: *Can I really do this? Will anyone care about what I have to say?*

Let me assure you: **You absolutely can, and your message matters.**

My Journey to Becoming an Author

It's 2020. The bandana covering my face feels like a poor excuse for a face mask. That's because it is. The real medical face masks have been sold out. I quickly run inside my apartment to make sure I don't bump into neighbors in my building, desperate not to breathe the same air as someone who may be, unknowingly, infected with COVID-19. Closing the door behind me I finally pull down the bandana off of my face.

Whew! Safe and alone. Alone. Alone with my inner thoughts and feelings. *I am not worthy. I'm a failure. Who would want to read my story? Is there anyone else struggling with these thoughts the way I am?* Plopping on my living room couch, I take a deep breath, lean my head back, look up, exhale slowly, and close my eyes. Silence, then a small quiet voice whispers: Write your story. Write the book and your story will help so many others.

It was during the height of COVID in the middle of New York City, that I felt an undeniable calling to share a deeply personal story: my journey through shame-based thinking. As an educator and perfectionism expert with over seven years of experience teaching at the graduate level, I was exploring the difference between guilt ("I made a mistake") and shame ("I am a mistake"). But my book wasn't born just from theory—it was born from my own raw, vulnerable experiences.

When I decided to write my first book, *I Slept with a Married Man: Am I Still a Good Person?* I encountered everything you might be feeling now: the deafening voices of self-doubt, external critics warning me to stay silent, and an overwhelming fear of rejection. But I also had something stronger—mentors, friends, and an unshakable belief that my story could make a difference.

Two years later, I held my published book in my hands. The results exceeded my wildest expectations:

- Appearances on **podcasts, a radio show, and TV shows.**
- Book tours in New York, Chicago, and Fort Lauderdale.
- Most importantly, **heartfelt conversations with readers** who saw themselves in my story and found hope.

It was during these book tours that a pattern began to emerge. After connecting over my story, people would pull me aside and ask, *"But how did you do it? How did you write and self-publish your book?"* These questions sparked the realization that this book—*Write It, Publish It, Sell It*—needed to exist.

Why *This* Book Exists

Writing and self-publishing a book can feel overwhelming. There's no shortage of guides that break down the process, but very few take you from the spark of an idea to becoming a **profitable, published author** who uses their book to open doors, grow their authority, and create new streams of income.

I learned how to do this through trial and error, and I've condensed those lessons into this comprehensive roadmap. In this book, you'll learn how to:

- Transform your idea into a finished manuscript.
- Navigate the publishing process with confidence.
- Position your book to reach your ideal readers.

- Build multiple income streams around your book.
- Establish yourself as an authority in your field.

This book is more than a guide—it's your personal publishing mentor.

The Reality Check

Let me be clear: writing and publishing a book is not a get-rich-quick scheme. The reality is sobering: the average book in the United States sells only 200 copies, and it often takes authors five years to move from idea to publication.

But here's the good news: **You're not average, and you don't have to take the average path.** With the right strategies and support, you can not only accelerate your journey but also achieve results beyond what you thought possible.

This book will help you avoid the common pitfalls that derail aspiring authors. It's packed with actionable steps, strategic insights, and real-world examples from my journey and the journeys of authors I've worked with through Janelle Villiers Partnerships (JVP) and at SayThat Publishing.

How to Use This Book

Whether you're starting with a spark of an idea or a partial manuscript, this book will meet you where you are. Each chapter builds on the last, guiding you step-by-step through the writing, publishing, and selling process. Along the way, you'll find exercises, worksheets, and practical advice to help you take immediate action.

This book also introduces you to SayThat Publishing's proven dual-editor approach—an innovative model that provides aspiring authors like you with **both content and grammar editing** for the price of one. Our mission is simple: to empower you to write, publish, and profit from your book without the overwhelm.

Let's Begin

If you're ready to turn your book dream into reality, this guide will be your blueprint. Together, we'll tackle your doubts, build a plan, and transform your message into something tangible, profitable, and impactful.

The journey begins here. Let's turn that dream inside you into a published book that inspires millions.

Chapter 1: Breaking Through the Barriers

Every aspiring author faces obstacles on their journey to publication. Doubts, time constraints, and financial concerns can feel like insurmountable barriers. But here's the truth: **every successful author started where you are now.**

The difference between those who publish and those who don't isn't talent—it's **action and the right support.** That's why **Janelle Villiers Partnerships (JVP)** & **SayThat Publishing**, don't just help authors get their books written and published; we provide a **step-by-step system** to turn your book into a powerful tool for impact, income, and authority.

This chapter is about identifying the biggest barriers to writing and publishing—and showing you how to overcome them with confidence, clarity, and expert support.

The Self-Doubt Trap

"What if no one wants to read my story?"
"Who am I to write this book?"
"Is my message worth sharing?"

If these thoughts sound familiar, you're not alone. Self-doubt is the **number one reason** many potential authors never start their books. I've worked with countless aspiring writers through workshops and coaching sessions, and I see it all the time—people with powerful messages who hesitate because they wonder if they're "qualified" to write a book.

Here's what I tell them: **your story matters precisely because it's yours.**

Think about a book that changed your life. What if that author had let self-doubt win? How many lives would remain untouched because they chose not to share their story? Right now, someone out there needs your book. They just don't know it yet.

This is why **Janelle Villiers Partnerships** & **SayThat Publishing** exists—to help authors **silence their doubts** and get their message into the world with professional, polished books that **command attention and build credibility.**

The Time Myth

"I'll write it when I have more time."
"I'm too busy right now."
"I'll get to it next year."

Time is one of the biggest myths that hold authors back. The average person takes five years to go from idea to publication—not because it actually takes that long, but because they wait for the "perfect time" that never comes.

At **Janelle Villiers Partnerships (JVP)** & **SayThat Publishing**, we help busy professionals, entrepreneurs, and thought leaders **bypass the struggle** by providing the structure, accountability, and expert guidance they need to get their book written faster.

Here's how we do it:
✅ **Proven writing frameworks** that simplify the process.
✅ **Professional editors** who refine your work, so you don't waste time over-editing.
✅ **Step-by-step publishing support** so you can focus on your message, not the technical details.

The truth is, you don't need vast amounts of free time—you need a system. Later in this book, I'll show you how dedicating just **30 minutes a day** can turn your dream into reality faster than you ever thought possible.

The Perfectionism Paralysis

As a perfectionism expert, I know how easy it is to get trapped in the mindset of "it has to be perfect before I share it." But let me tell you: **perfectionism is the enemy of progress.**

Novelist Jodi Picoult puts it perfectly: *"You can't edit a blank page."* Your first draft doesn't have to be perfect; it just has to exist. At **Janelle Villiers Partnerships (JVP)**, we tell our authors: **"Done is better than perfect. Perfect comes later."**

Think of your first draft as a conversation with yourself. It might be messy, but that's okay—it's the foundation you'll refine later. Progress, not perfection, will get your book published.

The Knowledge Gap

"I don't know how to publish a book."
"The process seems too complicated."
"I'm not sure where to start."

The publishing world can feel overwhelming. ISBNs, formatting, cover design, distribution—where do you even begin? This is where most aspiring authors get stuck.

The good news? **You don't have to figure it out alone.**

At **SayThat Publishing**, we simplify the entire process, handling everything from:
✅ **Professional book editing** (so your book is polished and reader-ready).
✅ **Custom cover design** (so your book looks just as good as its content).
✅ **Seamless distribution** to Amazon, Barnes & Noble, and global retailers.

We take care of the technical details, so you can focus on what matters—**sharing your message with the world.**

The Financial Concern

The costs associated with publishing can feel daunting, especially if you're considering self-publishing. But here's what most aspiring authors don't realize: those costs are manageable, and there are strategies to minimize them.

More importantly, I'll show you how to approach your book as an **investment** rather than just an expense. With the right positioning, your book can generate multiple income streams—transforming it into a long-term asset.

At **SayThat Publishing**, we help our authors turn their books into **business-building tools** that:

- **Position them as industry experts.**
- **Attract high-ticket clients and speaking gigs.**
- **Generate passive income** through multiple revenue streams.

Instead of just selling copies, we help authors **leverage their books for greater financial impact.** Whether that's launching a coaching business, securing media features, or booking paid speaking engagements, we make sure your book is **more than just pages—it's a strategy.**

Moving Forward: Your Action Plan

To break through these barriers and set yourself up for success, take these small but powerful steps:

1 **Acknowledge Your Doubts** – Write down your biggest fears about writing and publishing your book. Then, challenge each one with **evidence to the contrary.**

2 **Set a Minimum Viable Goal** – Start small. Commit to **15 minutes of writing per day** or **500 words per week.** Consistency beats perfection.

3 **Create Accountability** – Surround yourself with **people who believe in your book.** At **Janelle Villiers Partnerships (JVP)**, we offer expert guidance and a built-in support system to keep you on track.

4 **Start Where You Are** – Don't wait for the perfect moment. Begin outlining your book today. Use the exercises in the next chapter to clarify your message and set your book up for success.

You're Not Alone

Every successful author has faced these same challenges—but they didn't let them win. The difference between an *aspiring author* and a *published author* is simple: **published authors take action.**

At **Janelle Villiers Partnerships** & **SayThat Publishing**, we're here to **make that action easier** by giving you a clear path to writing, publishing, and profiting from your book.

Next Steps

In the next chapter, we'll dive into the **prewriting phase**, where you'll learn how to:
- ☑ Set crystal-clear goals for your book.
- ☑ Structure your content for maximum impact.
- ☑ Create a strategic plan that makes writing **effortless.**

Your book isn't just a dream—it's a reality waiting to happen. **Let's make it happen, together.**

Chapter 2: The Prewriting Phase: Setting Yourself Up for Success

Most aspiring authors make the mistake of diving straight into writing without a clear plan—only to find themselves stuck, overwhelmed, or unsure of their book's direction. However, **successful authors approach writing strategically.**

Before you write a single word, you need a blueprint that ensures your book **aligns with your goals, speaks to the right audience, and becomes a powerful asset for your brand or business.**

At **Janelle Villiers Partnerships (JVP)** and **SayThat Publishing**, we don't just help authors publish books—we help them build books that **work for them** long after launch. Whether your goal is to attract clients, establish yourself as an authority, or generate revenue, your book should be **designed with success in mind.**

This chapter will walk you through the **essential pre-writing steps** that will save you time, eliminate frustration, and position your book for maximum impact.

Maria's Journey: Finding Freedom Through Words

Maria stood at her office window, watching the city lights flicker as the sun dipped below the skyline. The **32nd floor** of her corporate building offered a breathtaking view, but tonight, all she could see was **another day slipping away.**

She had spent years coaching executives, **helping others build the careers and lives they dreamed of** while silently shelving her aspirations. She had knowledge that could transform people's lives, insights that deserved to be shared. But the thought of writing a book? That felt like **scaling a mountain without a map.**

She had tried before—scribbling notes on flights between conferences, jotting ideas in the margins of her planner. But the words never became more than scattered thoughts. **Where would she even start?**

One evening, as she sat at her kitchen table, while on a virtual meeting with me, as I coached her through speaking her dream out loud, she started thinking: *What if this book wasn't just a book?* What if it was the key to **a life she had only imagined?**

She grabbed a notebook and sketched out the details of her **ideal life.** Speaking internationally. Working with high-level corporate leaders who truly valued her expertise. **Making a difference** in how workplaces are built. And most importantly—**having dinner with her kids on a Tuesday evening instead of running another late-night workshop.**

Then she did the math.

She stared at the number in front of her—**$500,000.** That's what it would take for her to live this vision. She nearly choked on her coffee.

It felt impossible. Until it wasn't.

With the right strategy, Maria's book became **the foundation of something bigger than she had ever imagined.** Within a year of publishing, everything had changed. The Tuesday night dinners? They were no longer a dream. The international speaking engagements? She now chose **which continents she wanted to visit.** The financial freedom? That goal she thought was impossible?

She surpassed it by **year two.**

Looking back, Maria realized the greatest reward wasn't the numbers—it was **the lives she had changed, including her own.**

Dream Big: Setting Your Income Goals

Instead of starting with your book's content, I want you to start with your **dreams**.

Your book isn't just a collection of words—it's a **gateway to opportunities.**

Take a moment to imagine your **ideal life as an author**:
- ☑ Are you speaking at major events?
- ☑ Running transformative workshops?
- ☑ Traveling the world sharing your message?
- ☑ Building a coaching or consulting business?
- ☑ Creating passive income from book-related products?

Now, let's **put numbers to your dreams.**

When I did this exercise myself, I mapped out exactly what my dream lifestyle would cost. I wanted a **personal chef, business-class flights four times a year, and the freedom to focus on impactful work.** After crunching the numbers, I discovered my dream lifestyle required **$1.8 million annually**—significantly less than I initially thought.

This realization helped me understand that my book **couldn't just be a book—it had to be a business.**

Your Dream Income Exercise

1. **List everything you want in your ideal lifestyle.** Be specific.
2. **Research the actual costs of each item.**
3. **Calculate your total dream income.**
4. **Break this number down into monthly goals.**

Why is this important? Because understanding your financial and impact goals will shape **how you write, position, and market your book.**

Don't censor yourself during this exercise. Whether your number is $80,000 or $8 million, it's valid. The key is understanding exactly what you're working toward.

At **SayThat Publishing**, we specialize in helping authors create **business-driven books** that open doors to:

- Paid speaking engagements
- Coaching and consulting opportunities
- High-ticket workshops and courses
- Passive income through digital products

Your book is **more than words—it's a business asset.** And we're here to help you build it that way.

Understanding Book Income Streams

Many new authors assume book sales will be their main income stream. But here's a reality check:

📌 The average book sells **200–1,000 copies** in its lifetime.
📌 If you price your book at **$20** and earn a **50% royalty** ($10 per book), you'd need to sell **1,000 copies just to make $10,000.**

While direct sales are great, **they shouldn't be your only focus.**

Instead, the most successful authors use their books to **generate multiple streams of income.**

Here's how:

1. Speaking Engagements

✅ New speakers earn $500–$5,000 per event
✅ Experienced speakers charge $20,000–$50,000 per keynote
💡 Example: **Five speaking engagements at $2,000 each = $10,000**

Pro Tip: When negotiating speaking engagements, ask event organizers:
"Which charity would you like me to donate 10% of my book sales to?"

This simple question builds goodwill while increasing your **book sales and speaking fees.**

2. Coaching & Consulting

✅ Beginner coaches charge $1,000–$5,000 per client
✅ High-level consultants earn $50,000–$100,000 per client
💡 Example: **Five clients at $2,000 each = $10,000**

Your book positions you as an **expert** in your field, making it easier to attract high-paying clients.

3. Workshops & Programs

✅ Live workshops
✅ Online courses
✅ Group coaching programs
✅ VIP retreats

Your book can serve as the **foundation** for educational programs that bring in consistent revenue.

4. Book-Related Products

✅ Workbooks & journals
✅ Audiobooks & online courses
✅ Merchandise (shirts, mugs, planners)

Think of your book as a **launchpad** for an entire ecosystem of offerings.

Your book establishes you as an authority in your field, opening doors to these various income streams. Think of your book as a business card that pays you to distribute it.

Strategic Positioning

Before writing, you need to position your book strategically. Ask yourself:

1. **Who is my book for?** (Aspiring authors, entrepreneurs, coaches?)
2. **What problem does my book solve?**
3. **What transformation will my reader experience?**
4. **What action do I want them to take after reading?** (Hire me? Join my program?)

A well-positioned book isn't just informative—it's **transformational.**

Creating Your Book Blueprint

Now that you've defined your goals and audience, let's create your **book blueprint.**

Core Message Exercise

✅ **List the five key points** your readers must understand after reading your book.
✅ **Identify the three most crucial points.**
✅ **Determine the single most important takeaway.**

Success Metrics

- **Define what success looks like for your book.**
- Set **specific, measurable goals** for:

  - Book sales
  - Speaking engagements
  - Client acquisition
  - Media exposure

Timeline Creation

📅 **Set your publication target date.**
📅 Work backward to create **monthly milestones.**
📅 Schedule **consistent writing blocks.**

📌 **Pro Tip:** Many authors delay publishing because they lack accountability.
At **Janelle Villiers Partnerships (JVP)** & **SayThat Publishing**, we provide **built-in coaching, editorial guidance, and launch planning** to keep you on track.

Your Pre-Writing Checklist

Before moving to the writing phase, ensure you have:

- ☐ **Clearly defined income & impact goals**
- ☐ **Understanding of multiple revenue streams**
- ☐ **Identified target audience**
- ☐ **Crafted a Strategic book positioning**
- ☐ **Created a Comprehensive book blueprint**
- ☐ **Established a Publication timeline**
- ☐ **Set specific success metrics**

What's Next?

With your pre-writing foundation in place, you're now ready to start writing with clarity and confidence.

In the next chapter, we'll break down the **writing process** and show you how to:
📌 **Write consistently without feeling overwhelmed.**
📌 **Structure your book for maximum impact.**
📌 **Use proven techniques to stay motivated and on track.**

Your book is more than an idea—it's a **powerful tool waiting to be created.**

Let's bring it to life. 🚀

Chapter 3: The Writing Process – From Idea to Manuscript

Now that you have a **clear vision** for your book and a strategic blueprint in place, it's time for the part that separates aspiring authors from published ones: **writing.**

This is where most authors get stuck. They overthink, procrastinate, or feel overwhelmed by the sheer size of the task. But here's the truth: **writing a book is a process—not a one-time event.**

At **Janelle Villiers Partnerships (JVP)**, we help authors **ditch the overwhelm** by breaking the writing phase into simple, **manageable steps** that make progress inevitable.

If you've ever said…
❌ "I don't know where to start."
❌ "I don't have enough time."
❌ "I'm not a good writer."

…this chapter will change the way you see writing forever. Let's dive in.

The First Draft Mindset: Progress Over Perfection

Most people never finish their book because they expect their **first draft to be perfect.** That's a mistake.

Author Jodi Picoult says it best: *"You can always edit a bad page. You can't edit a blank one."*

Your first draft isn't supposed to be polished—it's supposed to exist. I want you to focus on getting through the **"messy first draft"** phase with one goal in mind: **progress, not perfection.**

Here's how to **release perfectionism** and get words on the page:

✔ **Think of your first draft as a brain dump.** No filters. No judgment. Just get your ideas out.

✔ **Write as if you're explaining it to a friend.** Keep it conversational and natural.

✔ **Skip sections you're stuck on.** You don't have to write in order—jump to what excites you.

✔ **Set time goals instead of word count goals.** (Example: 30 minutes of writing per session.)

At **SayThat Publishing**, we **refine, structure, and elevate** your work in the **editing phase**—but before we get there, your job is simply to **write without fear.**

Donley's Dawn: Finding Time in Life's Margins

"I don't have time."

For years, that was Donley's mantra. As a **manager for Atlanta's Number One restaurant,** while raising 2 young children, the idea of writing a book seemed **laughable.** His story existed **in his head, in scattered notes on his phone, in the advice he gave friends and colleagues daily**—but that's where it stayed.

Until he joined the Author's Voyage Course through Janelle Villiers Partnerships (JVP), everything changed. Where we outlined a plan to find time in his busy schedule to make his dream a reality.

"The first time I set my alarm for 5:45 AM, I thought I was crazy," Donley chuckles. *"My kids wouldn't be up until 6:45, and my wife thought I'd lost it. But there was something magical about those quiet morning moments—just me, my thoughts, and my laptop."*

Day by day, word by word, **his book took shape in the predawn quiet.** Some mornings, the words **flowed like coffee**; other days, it felt like **trudging through mud.** But he kept showing up—**thirty minutes at a time.**

Those minutes became **pages.**
The pages became **chapters.**
And within **90 days,** Donley held a **completed manuscript.**

"The beautiful part wasn't just finishing the book," he says, his voice warm with pride. *"It was showing my kids that dreams don't have to wait for 'someday.' They watched me write that book in the margins of life, and now my daughter wakes up early to work on her ideas and dreams, her story!"*

Donley didn't just write a book—**he rewrote what was possible.**

Creating a Writing Schedule That Works

One of the biggest myths about writing a book is that you need **large, uninterrupted blocks of time.** That's not true.

Instead of waiting for a **perfect day** to write, successful authors use **small, consistent writing sessions** to build momentum.

The 30-Minute Rule

⏱ **Write for 30 minutes per day.** (No distractions, no excuses.)
📅 **Commit to 5 days a week.** (Weekends off if you need them!)
📊 **Track your progress.** (Use a simple checklist or writing app.)

💡 **Real Results:** Writing for just **30 minutes a day, 5 days a week**, will give you:
📖 **10,000 words per month**
📖 **A completed first draft in 3-4 months**

At **Janelle Villiers Partnerships (JVP)**, we work with authors to set **custom writing plans** based on their schedules—whether they have **10 hours a week or just 10 minutes a day.**

Choosing Your Writing Approach: Time vs. Word Count Goals

Authors typically track progress in one of two ways:

🕐 **Time-Based Approach**
✔ Set a **daily writing time goal** (e.g., 30 minutes).
✔ Focus on **consistency over output**—just show up.
✔ Great for people who get overwhelmed by word counts.

📝 **Word-Based Approach**
✔ Set a **daily word count goal** (e.g., 500 words).
✔ Write until you **hit your target.**
✔ Great for goal-driven writers who like to measure progress.

💡 **Pro Tip:** If you're a perfectionist, use the **time-based method** so you're not obsessing over word count.

Structuring Your Book for Maximum Impact

To avoid **writer's block,** you need a **clear book structure.** Here's a simple way to organize your content:

📌 **The JVP Blueprint Method**
1 **Core Message:** What is the ONE big idea your book teaches?
2 **Key Points:** 3–5 main ideas that support your core message.
3 **Stories:** Personal experiences or examples that make your key points engaging.
4 **Action Steps:** Practical exercises that help readers apply what they've learned.

💡 **Example Breakdown:**
🟢 **Core Message:** "Self-publishing can be a profitable career path."
🟢 **Key Point 1:** Why traditional publishing isn't the only path.
🟢 **Key Point 2:** The financial potential of self-publishing.
🟢 **Key Point 3:** How to launch your book like a business.

- **Stories & Case Studies:** Real-life success stories of self-published authors.
- **Action Steps:** "Create a 90-day book launch plan."

At **Janelle Villiers Partnerships (JVP)**, we help authors refine **their book structure** so their message is **clear, engaging, and impactful.**

Overcoming Writer's Block: Proven Strategies

Feeling stuck? Try these **JVP-approved** strategies:

- **The Roll-the-Dice Method:** Struggling to start? Grab a die. Assign six different topics or questions to each number. Roll, and write about whatever comes up.
- **Voice Dictation:** Talk out your ideas and transcribe them later. (Great for people who think faster than they type!)
- **Write Out of Order:** Start with the **chapter that excites you most.** You don't have to write sequentially.
- **Switch Locations:** Stuck? Move to a different writing space—coffee shop, library, park.

At **Janelle Villiers Partnerships (JVP)**, we help authors **break through creative blocks** so they never feel stuck in the writing phase. Please refer to Appendix B for the "Roll-A-Story" worksheet.

Maintaining Momentum: Progress Tracking & Accountability

Staying consistent is easier when you **track progress and build accountability.**

- **Daily Writing Log:** Track your word count or minutes spent writing.
- **Weekly Completion Chart:** Set goals for finishing sections or chapters.
- **Monthly Milestones:** Break your book into manageable writing phases.

💡 **Pro Tip: Find an accountability partner or group.** Writers who share their goals with someone else are **65% more likely to finish their book.**

At **Janelle Villiers Partnerships (JVP)**, we provide **personalized coaching and writing accountability** to keep authors on track.

When Is Your First Draft "Done"?

Your first draft is complete when:
- ✔ **All key points are covered.**
- ✔ **The core message is clear.**
- ✔ **Basic structure is in place.**
- ✔ **Major stories are included.**
- ✔ **You've hit your word count goal (typically 40,000-60,000 words).**

Remember: Your **first draft won't be perfect,** but it will be **done.**

Once you reach this point, **SayThat Publishing** takes over with **our signature two-editor process**—where we transform your draft into a polished, professional book.

Next Steps: Moving to the Editing Phase

Your first draft is complete—now what? Here's what comes next:

📌 **Step 1:** Take a short break (1-2 weeks) before editing.
📌 **Step 2:** Do a **big-picture read-through** without making changes.
📌 **Step 3:** Make notes about any major fixes or missing content.
📌 **Step 4:** Prepare for **the professional editing phase.**

At **SayThat Publishing**, we guide authors through the entire **editing and refinement** process—so they **never feel lost or overwhelmed.**

What's Next?

In the next chapter, we'll explore the editing and refinement phase, including:
- ✅ The two types of editing your book needs.
- ✅ How to work with professional editors.
- ✅ What separates a good book from a great one.

Your book is written. Now let's make it exceptional. 🚀

Chapter 4: Editing & Refinement: Polishing Your Manuscript

Congratulations—you've written your first draft! That alone puts you ahead of **99% of aspiring authors.**

But writing is only half the journey. The difference between a **good book** and a **great book** comes down to **editing.**

Editing is where your manuscript evolves from **rough and unpolished** to **clear, engaging, and professional.** It's what ensures your book **resonates with readers, positions you as an authority, and sells.**

This chapter will guide you through the **editing process step by step**—what to expect, how to approach it, and what separates **a self-edited book from a professionally refined one.**

Jax's Revelation: The Power of Professional Editing

Jax still remembers the day she finished her first draft—the **pride of completion** quickly followed by **a wave of uncertainty.**

As a **successful mortgage broker, who majored in English in undergrad and went on to graduate from law school,** she was no stranger to writing. She had spent years polishing proposals, crafting high-stakes presentations, and delivering expert insights to clients. *"I thought I could edit it myself,"* she admits with a laugh. *"How different could a book be?"*

She quickly learned the answer: Hire a publishing company!

That's where **SayThat Publishing** was able to help her.

Her **content & development editor, Winston,** didn't just read her words—**he saw the potential between the lines.**

"Winston asked questions I hadn't even thought to ask myself, "Jax recalls. "He helped me uncover stories and insights I had taken for granted—things my readers needed to hear."

And I stepped in **as her grammar & line editor.** I used my attention to detail to transform her manuscript's **flow and readability.**

"It wasn't just about fixing commas," Jax explains. *"She helped my voice shine through—consistently, professionally, but still authentically me."*

Today, Jax's book continues to **open doors and create opportunities.**

"The investment in professional editing?" she reflects. *"It paid for itself. But the real return has been in the lives impacted. You can't put a price tag on that."*

◆　　◆　　◆

Have you ever picked up a book with:
🚩 Typos and grammar mistakes?
🚩 Awkward phrasing that made sentences hard to follow?
🚩 Ideas that felt repetitive or unorganized?

Chances are, you **didn't finish it.**

Readers expect books to be **polished and professional.** Even the most **brilliant ideas** will fall flat if they're buried under bad structure, confusing wording, or grammatical errors.

Your book deserves **the same level of refinement as traditionally published bestsellers.**

That's why successful authors don't edit alone.

The Two-Editor Advantage: Why Your Book Deserves the Best

One of the most valuable lessons I learned in my publishing journey was the power of **having two different types of editors.** Most authors assume editing is just about fixing typos—but it's so much more.

A **great book isn't just grammatically correct; it's structured, engaging, and compelling.** That's why **professional authors work with both a content & development editor and a grammar & line editor**—because each plays a crucial role in refining a manuscript.

Think of it like building a house:
🛠️ A **content & development editor** ensures the foundation is strong, the walls are in place, and the structure makes sense.
🎨 A **grammar & line editor** adds the finishing touches—the paint, trim, and decor that make everything look polished and professional.

While some editors offer **both services in one,** working with specialists often leads to **better results and a stronger final product.**

The Two Essential Types of Editing

1 Content & Development Editing (Big Picture)

A **content & development editor** focuses on:
✔ Overall message and flow
✔ Story structure and organization
✔ Clarity and readability
✔ Chapter sequencing
✔ Development of the plot and overall story
✔ Consistency of voice and tone
✔ Identifying missing information or weak sections

💡 **Goal:** Ensure your book is **clear, engaging, and well-structured.**

2 Grammar & Line Editing (The Final Polish)

A **grammar editor** focuses on:
✔ Sentence structure and grammar
✔ Word choice and phrasing
✔ Punctuation and spelling
✔ Formatting consistency
✔ Page layout and headings

💡 **Goal:** Make your book **error-free, easy to read, and professional.**

Many new authors try to **skip content editing and go straight to grammar fixes**—but this is a mistake. Even a **perfectly proofread book** won't sell if the structure, clarity, and flow aren't there.

The Editing Journey: Step-by-Step Process

📌 Stage 1: Self-Editing (1-2 Weeks)

Before sending your book to an editor, take time to **review and refine it yourself.**

* **Take a break.** Step away for at least **one week** before re-reading.
* **Read your book as a reader.** Highlight areas that feel unclear or repetitive.
* **Make big-picture revisions.** Cut fluff, strengthen weak sections, and refine your message.
* **List any concerns** you want feedback on from your editors.

📌 Stage 2: Content & Development Editing (2-4 Weeks)

This is where your book **gets its structure and clarity refined.**

* **Submit your manuscript for review.**
* **Receive feedback on flow, clarity, development, and structure.**
* **Schedule a feedback session to discuss changes.**

- Revise your book based on editor recommendations.
- Finalize content before moving to grammar editing.

📌 Stage 3: Grammar & Line Editing (2-3 Weeks)

Now, it's time for the **final polish**.

- Submit to a grammar & line editor.
- Review corrections on punctuation, sentence flow, and consistency.
- Ensure proper formatting and layout.
- Conduct a final proofread before moving to publishing.

By the end of this process, your book will be polished, professional, and ready for the world.

How Much Does Editing Cost?

*Editing is an **investment**—not an expense. A well-edited book **builds credibility, increases sales, and opens doors to speaking and business opportunities.***

📌 *Basic proofreading: $400–$800*
📌 *Line editing: $800–$1,600*
📌 *Content editing: $1,600–$3,000+*

💡 *Pro Tip: Budget for both types of editing. While some publishers **bundle content and grammar editing**, if you're going the independent route, you'll need to hire separate editors.*

How to Find the Right Editors The right editor can **elevate your book**—the wrong one can **change your voice or miss key issues.**

📌 Where to Look

- Professional editing associations
- Author communities & writing groups
- Publishing service providers
- Freelance platforms (Fiverr, Upwork, Reedsy)

📌 What to Look For

✔ Experience in your **genre**
✔ Understanding of your **target audience**
✔ Clear communication & availability
✔ Sample edit before committing
✔ References from other authors

💡 **Pro Tip:** The best editors **won't just fix errors—they'll challenge you to make your book better.**

Working Effectively with Editors

To get the most out of the editing process:

Before Editing Begins:

✅ Provide clear context about your book's goals and audience.
✅ Highlight specific concerns (e.g., "Does this chapter feel too long?").
✅ Set expectations for the **timeline and feedback style.**

During the Editing Process:

✅ **Stay open to feedback.** The goal is improvement, not criticism.
✅ **Ask questions** if you don't understand a suggested change.
✅ **Keep track of major edits** and document revisions.

After Receiving Edits:

☑ **Review all changes carefully** before accepting them.
☑ **Test readability** with beta readers for final feedback.
☑ **Save multiple versions** of your manuscript.

Editing can feel overwhelming, but **the right editor will be your biggest ally in creating a high-quality book.**

Common Editing Challenges (and How to Overcome Them)

📌 **Emotional Reactions:** It's normal to feel overwhelmed by feedback. Take time to process suggestions before reacting.
📌 **Too Many Changes:** Focus on the edits that truly **enhance clarity and impact.**
📌 **Perfectionism:** No book is ever "perfect." Aim for **polished and professional** instead.

💡 **Editing isn't about changing your voice—it's about making your message stronger.**

Final Quality Check: Is Your Book Ready?

Before moving to publishing, ask yourself:

✔ **Is every chapter clear and engaging?**
✔ **Does your book have a logical flow?**
✔ **Is the grammar and sentence structure clean?**
✔ **Are all formatting elements (headings, page numbers, citations) correct?**
✔ **Have beta readers given final feedback?**

🚀 If you can check **all these boxes**, your book is officially **ready for the world!**

What's Next? Moving to Publishing

*Editing is complete—now comes the exciting part: **bringing your book to life.***

In the next chapter, we'll dive into:
📌 *The **different publishing options** (self-publishing vs. traditional).*
📌 ***How to get your book listed on Amazon, Barnes & Noble, and beyond.***
📌 *The **step-by-step process of turning your manuscript into a published book.***

*Your book is polished, professional, and **ready for the world.** Now, let's get it in the hands of readers!* 🚀

In the next chapter, we'll explore the publishing process and how to choose the right publication path for your book.

Chapter 5: Publishing Strategy – Choosing Your Path to Success

Sophie's Publishing Journey: Finding the Right Path

Sophie's hands trembled as she hit **save** on the final draft of *Breaking Free: A Survivor's Guide to Overcoming Workplace Bullying.*

As a former **HR executive** who had endured **harassment firsthand,** this book wasn't just a project—it was **her life's purpose, distilled into 65,000 words.**

"Each chapter felt like I was reliving those moments," Sophie shares, her voice softening. *"The panic attacks in the bathroom between meetings, the sleepless nights, the journey to reclaiming my power. I knew there were others out there feeling just as alone as I had."*

But after pouring her heart into the manuscript, **uncertainty crept in.**

For three months, the file sat untouched on her computer while she wrestled with **how to publish it.**

Traditional publishers wanted to **water down her message**, making it *"less confrontational."* But **self-publishing alone felt overwhelming.**

"I had nightmares about typos on the back cover," she admits with a laugh.

Then, she found the **right path.**

Working with **SayThat Publishing**, her **anxiety turned into action.** Her book launched—and the results were bigger than she ever imagined.

✨ **#1 in three categories** – Workplace Culture, Business Ethics, and Professional Development
✨ **500 copies sold in the first month**
✨ **Invited to speak at 3 Fortune 500 companies**
✨ **Generated $75,000 in consulting contracts**

But the **real impact** came from the people who needed her book the most.

"The book became more than my story—it became a movement," Sophie says. *"We're now developing corporate training programs, and I've helped five other survivors publish their stories. Last week, a reader told me my book gave her the courage to file a formal complaint and seek therapy. That's when I knew—every tear I shed writing this book was worth it."*

Sophie didn't just write a book. **She changed lives.**

◆　　◆　　◆

Your manuscript is polished and ready—now comes the **big question:** how will you publish it?

With more publishing options available than ever before, it's crucial to choose the **right path** based on your **goals, timeline, and level of involvement.**

This chapter will walk you through the **two primary publishing paths—traditional vs. self-publishing—**along with the best platforms, pricing strategies, and essential steps to get your book into readers' hands.

Traditional vs. Self-Publishing: Understanding Your Options

For decades, **traditional publishing** was the only way to get a book into bookstores. Today, self-publishing has created **a new level of freedom and opportunity for authors.**

Let's break down the key differences:

Traditional Publishing

✅ **Pros:**
✔ No upfront costs—publisher covers editing, design, and printing.
✔ Publisher handles production and distribution.
✔ Potential to receive an **advance payment** for your book.
✔ Established **bookstore and library distribution channels.**

❌ **Cons:**
✖ **Lower royalties** (typically 4-8%).
✖ **Long timeline**—can take **1-3 years** from acceptance to release.
✖ **Limited creative control**—publishers **control cover design, edits, and pricing.**
✖ **Difficult to get a deal**—requires a literary agent and strong sales potential.

💡 **Best for:** Authors who want a **prestigious publisher name behind their book** and are **willing to trade control for industry backing.**

Self-Publishing

✅ **Pros:**
✔ **Higher royalties** (40-70%)—you keep more of your earnings.
✔ **Faster time to market**—you control the timeline.
✔ **Complete creative control**—you decide the cover, format, and content.

✔ **Guaranteed publication**—no gatekeepers rejecting your work.
✔ **Ownership of rights**—no one controls your book but you.

❌ **Cons:**
✖ **Upfront costs**—editing, cover design, and distribution are your responsibility.
✖ **Marketing is on you**—without a publisher, you **must build your audience.**
✖ **Limited bookstore access**—most physical retailers prefer traditionally published books.

💡 **Best for:** Authors who want **full control, higher royalties, and a faster publishing process**—especially those with a **business, coaching, or speaking platform.**

Which Path is Right for You?

Ask yourself:

📌 **Do I want complete control over my book, or am I okay with a publisher making decisions?**
📌 **Do I want to publish quickly, or am I willing to wait years for a deal?**
📌 **Am I comfortable investing in professional editing and design, or do I need a publisher to cover costs?**
📌 **Am I ready to market my book myself, or do I want publisher support?**

💡 **Pro Tip: You can always start with self-publishing and transition to traditional later. Many authors use self-publishing to build an audience and attract publishing deals down the road.**

Understanding Self-Publishing Platforms

If you choose to self-publish, selecting the **right platform** is key. Let's break down the most popular options:

Amazon KDP (Kindle Direct Publishing)

📌 **Best for:** Authors who want **direct access to Amazon's massive audience.**
📌 **Key benefits:**
✔ Largest online bookstore.
✔ Print and digital options (paperback, Kindle, and hardcover).
✔ Fast publishing—books go live within **24–72 hours.**
✔ No upfront cost (but printing costs are deducted per sale).

⚠ **Limitations:**

- **Amazon-focused**—doesn't distribute widely to bookstores.
- If you enroll in **KDP Select**, Amazon **requires exclusivity for eBooks.**

IngramSpark

📌 **Best for:** Authors who want **bookstore distribution and high-quality printing.**
📌 **Key benefits:**
✔ **Global distribution** to **Barnes & Noble, Target, libraries, and indie bookstores.**
✔ **Superior print quality**—better paper, cover finishes, and binding.
✔ **Hardcover options** (Amazon KDP doesn't offer dust jackets).

⚠ **Limitations:**

- **Upfront setup costs** (print fees for author copies).
- **No built-in Amazon promotion tools** like KDP Select.

Other Self-Publishing Platforms

📌 **Draft2Digital** – Great for **wide eBook distribution (Apple, Nook, Kobo).**

📌 **Lulu** – Best for **workbooks, journals, and specialty books.**

📌 **Barnes & Noble Press** – Good for **US-based print distribution.**

💡 **Pro Tip:** Many authors use **a hybrid approach**—publishing through **Amazon KDP for Amazon sales** and **IngramSpark for bookstore distribution.**

Choosing the Right Publishing Platform

Not all publishing platforms are the same—choosing the **right one** depends on your **distribution goals, print quality needs, and financial considerations.**

Here's what to evaluate before making your decision:

📌 Distribution Goals

Consider where you want your book to be available:

✅ Do you want **Amazon exclusivity, or do you prefer wide distribution**?

✅ Is having your book **in bookstores** a priority?

✅ Do you want to sell **internationally**?

✅ Is **library access** important for your book's audience?

✅ Will you sell books **directly at events or from your website**?

💡 **Amazon KDP dominates online sales, but IngramSpark provides access to bookstores, libraries, and global retailers.**

📌 Quality Considerations

Not all platforms offer the same **printing standards.** Think about:
✅ **Paperback vs. hardcover options** (Amazon KDP limits hardcover choices).
✅ **Cover finish preferences** (glossy vs. matte).
✅ **Paper quality and color vs. black & white interior.**
✅ **Binding options** (perfect bound, case laminate, dust jacket).

💡 **IngramSpark offers superior print quality** and more **formatting options** compared to Amazon KDP.

📌 Financial Considerations

Each platform has different **cost structures, royalty models, and distribution fees.** Consider:
✅ **Upfront setup costs** – Some platforms charge fees while others don't (Amazon KDP and IngramSpark).
✅ **Per-book printing costs** – These vary by **page count, color vs. black & white, and format.**
✅ **Shipping expenses** – Important if you plan to **sell books directly.**
✅ **Return policies** – Bookstores **require returnable books,** but this adds costs.
✅ **Royalty payments** – How and when you get paid for book sales.

💡 **Amazon KDP is free to set up,** but **IngramSpark charges fees for better bookstore distribution.**

The Hybrid Approach: Why Many Authors Use Multiple Platforms

Many successful authors don't **limit themselves to one platform**—instead, they use a **hybrid strategy** to maximize their reach.

📌 **Amazon KDP** – Best for selling on **Amazon** with fast publishing and high royalties.

📌 **IngramSpark** – Ideal for **bookstore distribution, libraries, and high-quality print options and eBook distribution** to Nook, Apple Books, and more

📌 **Direct Sales** – Selling through **your website, events, and speaking engagements** gives you **higher profits per book.**

📌 **Draft2Digital / Smashwords** – Expand your **eBook distribution** to Apple Books, Kobo, and more.

💡 **By combining platforms, you get the best of both worlds—Amazon's reach AND bookstore availability.**

Final Takeaway: What's Your Best Choice?

🚀 If your goal is **fast online sales with no setup fees**, start with **Amazon KDP.**

🚀 If you want to be **in bookstores and libraries**, use **IngramSpark** for wide distribution.

🚀 If you plan to **sell at events or in bulk**, consider **ordering directly from IngramSpark or a printing service.**

🚀 If you want **eBooks on multiple platforms**, use **IngramSpark, Draft2Digital, or Smashwords** alongside KDP.

By choosing the **right mix of platforms,** you can **maximize sales, exposure, and opportunities** for your book.

Publishing Package Essentials

To publish professionally, **your book needs more than just a manuscript.**

Basic Publishing Requirements

- ISBN & barcode (identifies your book worldwide).
- Copyright registration (protects your work legally).
- Professional cover design (first impressions matter).
- Interior formatting (for clean print & digital reading).
- Proof copies (check print quality before mass release).

Optional Add-Ons

- Audiobook version (expands your audience).
- Digital formatting (for Kindle, Nook, iBooks).
- Foreign rights (translate and sell worldwide).
- Multiple formats (paperback, hardcover, eBook).

Working with a Publishing Service: Should You Go Solo or Get Expert Help?

Navigating the publishing process alone can be overwhelming. Between **editing, formatting, ISBNs, printing, distribution, and marketing,** the amount of detail involved can make even the most motivated author feel stuck.

That's why many authors choose to work with a **full-service publishing partner**—to **eliminate stress, save time, and ensure a professional-quality book.**

However, not all publishing services are created equal. If you're considering **working with a publishing partner,** it's important to choose wisely.

What to Look for in a Publishing Service

Before committing to a publishing service, ensure they provide:

✅ **Transparent pricing** – No hidden fees or surprise costs.
✅ **Clear communication** – They guide you through each step.
✅ **Proven industry expertise** – Experience in your genre and market.
✅ **Robust quality control** – Professional **editing, formatting, and design.**
✅ **Marketing & launch support** – A clear plan to help you sell books.
✅ **Rights retention** – **You keep 100% ownership of your book.**
✅ **Flexible distribution** – Ability to **sell on Amazon, bookstores, and beyond.**

💡 **Beware of vanity publishers** that charge high fees upfront but offer **little real distribution or marketing support.**

The Benefits of a Full-Service Publishing Partner

Many successful authors **don't do everything alone.** They work with **trusted professionals** who handle the technical aspects so they can **focus on writing and growing their brand.**

Here's what a full-service publishing partner can do for you:

📌 **Comprehensive Care** – Everything from **editing to distribution** is handled by one team.
📌 **Dual-Editor Approach** – Ensures both **content and grammar editing** for a polished final product.
📌 **High-Quality Printing** – Access to **premium print options** for a professional look.
📌 **Rights Protection** – **You retain full ownership** and control over pricing and sales.
📌 **Marketing Guidance** – Expert advice on **positioning, launch**

strategies, and branding.

📌 **Time-Saving Process** – Skip the frustration of **figuring it all out alone.**

📌 **Cost-Effective Packages** – Bundled services often save money vs. hiring separately.

📌 **Global Distribution** – Ability to sell on **Amazon, bookstores, and international markets.**

For authors who want **a professional book without the stress of DIY publishing,** a **trusted publishing service** can make all the difference.

DIY vs. Full-Service: Which Is Right for You?

📌 **Go DIY if...**

✔ You want **full control** and are willing to learn the entire process.

✔ You have time to **research, manage, and coordinate** all publishing steps.

✔ You're comfortable handling **ISBNs, formatting, and marketing yourself.**

📌 **Consider a publishing partner if...**

✔ You want a **stress-free, expert-guided** publishing experience.

✔ You want to **focus on writing and business growth** instead of logistics.

✔ You need professional **editing, formatting, and marketing support.**

💡 **Your book is a reflection of you—investing in quality can make all the difference in its success.**

Final Thought: Make the Choice That Fits Your Goals

Whether you choose to **publish independently or work with a team,** your goal should be the same:
📖 A **professionally edited, beautifully designed, and well-positioned** book.

If you're considering **working with a publishing partner,** take your time, ask questions, and ensure they align with **your goals, budget, and vision.**

🚀 **Next up: How to market and launch your book for maximum success!**

Making the Smart Publishing Choice

When I wrote my first book, I had to **figure everything out alone**—from hiring editors to choosing distribution channels to ensuring my book met industry standards.

It was **time-consuming, expensive, and often overwhelming.** I made mistakes, spent money where I didn't need to, and learned the hard way that **publishing isn't just about writing—it's about strategy.**

This experience made me realize that **many authors struggle not because they lack talent, but because they lack a roadmap.** That's why having a clear publishing plan—and the right support—can make all the difference.

Quality Control: Setting Your Book Up for Success

Readers judge books by their **professionalism, readability, and overall experience.** Before hitting "publish," ensure your book meets industry standards.

📌 Print Quality Checklist

✅ High-resolution **cover design** (first impressions matter!).
✅ Proper **interior formatting** for readability.
✅ Quality **paper stock** and binding strength.
✅ Accurate **color reproduction** for images.
✅ Consistent **fonts, margins, and layout.**

📌 Digital Quality Checklist

✅ Correct **file formats** (EPUB, MOBI, PDF).
✅ Compatibility across **Kindle, Apple Books, and other eReaders.**
✅ Linked **table of contents** for navigation.
✅ High-resolution images and **clean layout.**
✅ Accurate **metadata** to optimize searchability.

💡 **Pro Tip:** Even small formatting errors **can make a book feel unprofessional.** Taking time for quality control ensures **positive reader experiences and strong reviews.**

Pricing Strategy: How to Price Your Book for Profit & Reach

Your book's price affects **sales, reader perception, and overall profitability.**

📖 Print Book Pricing – Consider:

📌 **Production costs** – Printing, shipping, and fees.
📌 **Market standards** – Competitive pricing in your genre.
📌 **Profit margins** – How much you keep per sale.
📌 **Retail pricing strategies** – Discounts and bulk pricing.

💡 **Typical Range:**

- Paperbacks: **$12.99 – $19.99**
- Hardcovers: **$24.99 – $34.99**

📱 eBook Pricing – Consider:

📌 Market norms for your genre.
📌 Reader price sensitivity (cheaper books sell more).
📌 Promotional pricing strategies (e.g., $0.99 launch promotions).

💡 **Typical Range:**

- eBooks: **$2.99 – $9.99**

💡 **Pro Tip:** Lower eBook pricing can boost **sales volume, rankings, and visibility**—especially during launch.

Preparing for Launch: The Final Steps

A **successful book launch** doesn't happen by accident. Before publishing, ensure you have:

📌 **ISBNs & copyright registration** secured.
📌 **Finalized metadata** (title, keywords, categories).
📌 **Professional cover & formatting** locked in.
📌 **Marketing materials** (press kits, social media assets).
📌 **Author platforms ready** (website, social media, Amazon author page).
📌 **Launch timeline planned** (pre-orders, promotions, review strategy).

💡 **Pro Tip:** Ordering **proof copies** before launch helps catch last-minute errors and ensures your book **looks and feels right.**

Post-Publication: Managing & Growing Your Book's Success

Publishing isn't the finish line—it's the **beginning** of your book's journey.

📌 After Launch Checklist

✅ **Monitor sales & rankings** across platforms.
✅ **Track reader feedback & reviews.**
✅ **Adjust pricing** based on market trends.
✅ **Update metadata** (categories, keywords) for better discoverability.
✅ **Schedule ongoing promotions** to keep sales strong.

💡 **Books that continue selling long-term** are the ones that **stay visible and relevant.**

Moving Forward: Your Publishing Strategy Matters

Your publishing approach should align with your **long-term career and financial goals.** Whether you:

📌 Want to build **a brand and business** around your book...

📌 Want your book in **stores, libraries, and global markets**...

📌 Need expert **guidance to avoid costly mistakes**...

...choosing the right **publishing strategy** can be the difference between **a book that sits unnoticed** and one that **sells, impacts, and opens doors.**

Publishing **doesn't have to be overwhelming**—with the right plan (and the right support), you can bring your book to life **without the stress.**

🚀 **Next up: How to market and launch your book for maximum visibility and sales!**

Chapter 6: Marketing & Promotion – Building Your Bestseller

Joshua's Marketing Breakthrough

Joshua had spent **fifteen years as a cybersecurity expert,** comfortable in the world of **firewalls, encryption, and risk mitigation.** But when it came to marketing his book, he felt **completely exposed.**

"I'm the guy who declined speaking at industry conferences because the spotlight terrified me," he confesses. *"My wife actually laughed when I mentioned social media marketing. She'd been trying to get me on Facebook for years."*

After meeting with **SayThat Publishing,** who explained that without visibility, even the **most brilliant book** can sit unread.

Joshua decided to try the **breadcrumbing strategy, they recommended,** starting small—just a **daily insight** to share his knowledge.

📅 **Day 1:** A simple **coffee cup photo with his laptop** → *5 likes.*
📅 **Week 1:** A personal story about his **first cyber attack** → *100+ shares.*
📅 **Month 1:** A video explaining **encryption to his 5-year-old** → *Went viral with 50,000 views.*
📅 **Launch Week: 15,000 followers across platforms.**

*"The response was staggering. Each post sparked conversations. CIOs started reaching out privately. One post about password security turned into a **$20,000 consulting contract.**"*

By the end of the first year, the results were undeniable:

- 📖 **Book Sales:** 2,000 copies
- 🎤 **Speaking Fees:** $80,000 (8 events)
- 💼 **Consulting Contracts:** $150,000
- 💻 **Online Course Sales:** $30,000
- 📊 **Total Revenue: $260,000+**

But **the numbers weren't the most important part.**

"Last month, a small nonprofit wrote to thank me," Joshua says, wiping away unexpected tears. *"They had implemented my security protocols after reading my book. Two weeks later, they stopped a ransomware attack that would have destroyed them."*

At that moment, Joshua realized—**this wasn't about marketing anymore.**

This was about **protection and empowerment.**

◆ ◆ ◆

Your book is written, published, and ready to launch—but **how do you make sure people actually buy it?**

Marketing is the **key** to turning your book from just another title on Amazon into a **bestseller that drives long-term sales, opportunities, and influence.**

This chapter will guide you through **proven book marketing strategies, launch planning, and ongoing promotion techniques** to build momentum, sell more books, and **position yourself as an authority in your field.**

The Bestseller Strategy: A Proven Approach

Achieving **bestseller status** isn't about luck—it's about **strategy.**

Take author Jacqueline Crider, for example. Her book, *Mortgage 101: The Secret Sauce of Home Buying*, hit **#1 on Amazon** because of a carefully **orchestrated launch strategy.**

The formula? **Optimized categories, strategic pre-orders, and a structured marketing plan.**

Here's how you can do the same.

Understanding Amazon Categories: The Hidden Key to #1

Many authors don't realize that **Amazon rankings are based on category sales.**

By choosing **specific, less competitive categories,** you can increase your chances of hitting **#1 faster.**

Example Category Requirements

📖 **Broad Category (History > Biographies)**

- **#1 Spot:** Requires **395** books sold
- **Bestseller Badge:** Requires **16** books sold

📖 **Niche Category (History > Biographies > UK)**

- **#1 Spot:** Requires **4** books sold
- **Bestseller Badge:** Requires **1** book sold

💡 **Pro Tip:** Choosing a **niche category** allows you to **reach #1 with fewer sales** while still appearing in broader category searches.

How to Pick the Right Categories

✅ **Browse Amazon's category lists** and find relevant niches.
✅ **Check how many books are selling** in your target category.
✅ **Select categories where you can realistically compete.**
✅ **Use pre-orders to boost first-day sales ranking.**

🚀 **Authors who plan their categories strategically** increase their chances of hitting **bestseller lists** and gaining visibility.

The Breadcrumb Marketing Method: Building Pre-Launch Hype

The most successful book launches don't **start on launch day—they start months before.**

Marketing your book **before it's published** builds momentum and ensures **strong launch-day sales.**

Real-World Pre-Launch Success Stories

📖 **Author Sarah M.'s Journey**
✅ **Week 1:** Shared a **photo of her outline** → 500+ likes
✅ **Week 4:** Posted **beachside writing session** → Featured in a writing community
✅ **Week 8:** Did a **cover reveal** → 2,000+ shares
✅ **Week 12:** Hosted a **pre-launch event** → Sold 200 pre-orders

📖 **Author Marcus T.'s Strategy**
✅ Created a **writing progress tracker** → Went viral in author groups
✅ Shared **early morning writing routine** → Picked up by productivity bloggers
✅ Posted **editing session clips** → Generated **editing service inquiries**
✅ **Launch day celebration** → Reached **#1 in three categories**

💡 The takeaway? Consistency and storytelling sell books.

Content Ideas That Convert

The best book marketing isn't **salesy—it's engaging.** Here's what to post:

📅 Weeks 1-4: Writing Phase

📌 Share **your outline or sticky notes on a wall.**
📌 Post **your writing workspace or favorite writing spot.**
📌 Document **your daily writing progress.**

📅 Weeks 5-8: Editing Phase

📌 Post **chapter completion updates.**
📌 Share a **milestone celebration (hitting 20,000 words, finishing draft, etc.).**
📌 Show a **glimpse into your editing process.**

📅 Weeks 9-12: Pre-Launch Hype

📌 **Cover reveal!** (Make it a big moment.)
📌 Share **endorsements or early reader feedback.**
📌 Announce **pre-orders and incentives.**
📌 Start a **launch countdown.**

🚀 Each post builds anticipation and turns followers into buyers.

Launch Phase Marketing: Maximizing Your Book's Visibility

📌 Your Digital Presence Matters

✅ **Author Website** – A simple **landing page with your book, bio, and links.**

✅ **Book Landing Page** – Include **a sample chapter and pre-order links.**
✅ **Media Kit** – Press materials for **podcasts, blogs, and interviews.**

📌 Social Media Strategies

✅ **Daily Updates** – Writing progress, behind-the-scenes, and reader engagement.
✅ **Live Sessions** – Share insights, answer questions, and **talk about your book.**
✅ **Reader Engagement** – Ask questions, get feedback, and build community.

📌 Email Marketing

✅ **Exclusive Launch Sequences** – Announce book releases, bonuses, and events.
✅ **Bonus Content** – Free PDFs, behind-the-scenes access, or signed copies.
✅ **Early Bird Offers** – Special pricing for pre-orders.

🚀 **A strong online presence ensures your book stays visible long after launch.**

Leveraging Media Coverage & Speaking Engagements

Getting media exposure boosts **credibility, reach, and book sales.**

📌 Press Releases & Media Outreach

✅ Announce **your book launch, milestones, and impact stories.**
✅ Pitch yourself for **podcast interviews, radio segments, and guest articles.**

📌 Speaking Engagements That Sell Books

📖 **Industry conferences**
📖 **Local events & workshops**
📖 **Podcast guest spots**

💡 **Pro Tip:** When booking **speaking gigs,** ask:
"Which charity would you like me to donate 10% of book sales to?"
This increases book sales while supporting a good cause.

Turning Your Book into a Business: Multiple Income Streams

Your book can be more than just **royalties**—it can lead to **high-ticket opportunities.**

📌 Speaking Circuit

✅ **Conference keynotes**
✅ **Corporate training**
✅ **Workshop facilitation**

💡 **Typical Speaking Fees**
🗣 **New Speakers:** $500 – $5,000 per event
🗣 **Experienced Speakers:** $20,000 – $50,000 per event

📌 Consulting & Coaching

✅ **One-on-one coaching**
✅ **Group programs**
✅ **Online courses**

💡 **Typical Coaching Rates**
👥 **Beginner Coaches:** $1,000 – $5,000 per client
👥 **Experienced Coaches:** $50,000+ per client

🚀 Your book is a lead magnet that attracts high-paying opportunities.

Measuring Success: Tracking Growth & Scaling Impact

The best authors **track their success and adjust strategies.**

📌 Key Metrics to Track

✅ **Book sales** and **Amazon rankings**
✅ **Speaking engagement bookings**
✅ **Media appearances** (TV, podcasts, blogs)
✅ **Social media engagement & email list growth**
✅ **ROI from marketing efforts**

📌 Scaling Beyond the Launch

✅ **Create ongoing content** (blog posts, videos, email newsletters).
✅ **Engage with readers in online communities.**
✅ **Plan future books, events, and collaborations.**

🚀 A great book isn't just launched—it's consistently marketed.

Final Thought: Marketing Is an Ongoing Process

Marketing isn't just about **selling books—it's about building a brand, creating opportunities, and growing your platform.**

📌 **Be consistent.** Small daily efforts add up.
📌 **Be authentic.** Share your journey—people connect with real stories.

📌 **Add value.** Help readers, entertain, or inspire them.
📌 **Build relationships.** The stronger your network, the better your sales.

🚀 **Next up: Long-term author success and leveraging your book beyond its launch!**

🚀 *Ready to become a bestselling author?*

At **SayThat Publishing**, *we specialize in turning books into bestsellers with **proven launch strategies, targeted marketing, and expert guidance.***

*Becoming a **bestselling author** isn't just about ranking #1—it's about **creating impact, building authority, and unlocking new opportunities.** With the right **strategy, positioning, and ongoing promotion,** your book can become a powerful tool for long-term success.*

*If you're looking for a **team that understands the business of books**, we're here to help. Let's work together to **launch, market, and scale your book for success.***

✉️ ***Want to learn more?** Contact **Janelle Villiers Partnerships (JVP)** & **SayThat Publishing** today and discover how we can help you achieve your publishing and marketing goals: janelle@jvillierspartnerships.com*

Chapter 7: Building Your Author Empire – Maximizing Your Book's Potential

Writing a book is an achievement—but turning it into an **author empire** is where the real impact and financial success begin.

A book isn't just a product. **It's a business foundation, a credibility booster, and a gateway to high-income opportunities.**

This chapter will show you how to:
- ☑ **Leverage your book for speaking, coaching, and consulting**
- ☑ **Create multiple revenue streams from a single book**
- ☑ **Use your expertise to build a sustainable, profitable brand**

Let's dive into real-world success stories, step-by-step strategies, and proven models to maximize your book's potential.

Real-World Success Stories: Beyond Book Sales

A book can do more than generate royalties—it can open doors to **high-paying clients, speaking engagements, and business opportunities.**

My Journey: How My Book Created a Business

When I published *I Slept with a Married Man: Am I Still a Good Person?* I sold approximately **250 copies**. While those sales were meaningful, the real financial impact came from **leveraging my book into a business.**

📍 **3 Book Tour Stops** (New York, Chicago, Fort Lauderdale)
🎙️ **Multiple Podcast Interviews**
📺 **TV Show Appearance**
📻 **Radio Features**
🎤 **Speaking Engagements**
💼 **Coaching Clients**

📊 **Total Revenue Generated: Over $20,000** through:
✔ Consulting/Coaching Services
✔ Speaking Fees
✔ Workshop Facilitation
✔ Author Coaching
✔ Book-Related Opportunities

Your book is **a launchpad**—when positioned correctly, it can create **six-figure business opportunities.**

Success Stories

📖 **Sarah M – Leadership Coach**
💡 *Initial book sales: 200+ copies*
📊 **Business Growth:**
✔ 12 Paid Speaking Opportunities
✔ 3 Corporate Training Contracts
📈 **Revenue Breakdown:**
✔ Speaking: **$35,000**
✔ Corporate Training: **$75,000**
✔ Individual Coaching: **$40,000**
🎯 **Total Impact: $150,000+ in 18 months**

📖 **Marcus T – Wellness Author**
💡 *Created an online course and membership program*
📊 **Revenue Streams:**
✔ Online Course: **200 students = $60,000**
✔ Membership Site: **150 members = $45,000/year**
✔ Consulting: **$30,000**
✔ Speaking: **$25,000**
🎯 **Total Annual Impact: $160,000+**

Creating Your $10K+ Book Strategy

Your book isn't just a **standalone product**—it's a **business asset.** Here's how to generate **$10,000+ from your book beyond direct sales.**

1 Direct Book Sales

☑️ **Royalties:** Earn **50% of the retail price** (self-publishing).
☑️ **Bulk Orders:** Sell books in **large quantities at events.**
☑️ **Live Sales:** Sign and sell books at **conferences, workshops, and coaching programs.**

💡 **Example Calculation:**
📖 200 books × **$10 royalty = $2,000**

2 Paid Speaking Engagements

A book makes you **instantly credible** as a speaker.

📊 **Speaking Fee Progression:**
🎤 Beginner: **$500 – $2,500** per event
🎤 Established: **$5,000 – $15,000** per event
🎤 Expert Level: **$20,000 – $50,000** per keynote

💡 **Success Stories:**
📖 **James R.** → First **paid speech 30 days post-launch** ($2,500).
📖 **Rebecca M.** → **Corporate training contract** ($25,000).
📖 **Mark T.** → **International keynote** ($15,000).

🚀 **Pro Tip:** Use your book as a **lead magnet** to get paid speaking gigs faster.

3 High-Ticket Consulting & Coaching

Many readers want **personalized guidance**—and they're willing to pay for it.

📊 **Client Success Stories:**
📖 Leadership Author: **5 clients × $5,000 each = $25,000**
📖 Health Expert: **Group program = $50,000/quarter**
📖 Business Strategist: **Corporate consulting = $100,000+**

🚀 **Your book attracts high-ticket clients who trust your expertise.**

4 Digital Product Suite

📚 **Online Courses** – Expand your book's content into **video lessons & group coaching.**
💻 **Membership Communities** – Offer **exclusive content, live Q&As, and ongoing support.**
🏢 **Corporate Training Programs** – Sell workshops to **businesses and organizations.**

📊 **Example Pricing:**
✅ Online Course: **$297 – $997**
✅ Monthly Membership: **$25 – $250 per month**
✅ Corporate Workshops: **$5,000 – $50,000+**

🚀 **Your book is just the beginning—turn it into an ecosystem of income streams.**

Leveraging Your Authority for More Opportunities

📌 Media Exposure & Brand Partnerships

✅ Paid Contributor Roles (Forbes, Business Insider, etc.)
✅ Podcast Features & Guest Articles
✅ Expert Commentary on Industry Trends
✅ Sponsored Content & Product Collaborations

💡 **Media makes you more valuable—every interview increases credibility.**

Your Multi-Stream Revenue Plan

📊 Example Monthly Revenue Mix:

Income Stream	Monthly Revenue 💰
Book Royalties	$1,000
Speaking (2 events)	$5,000
Consulting (3 clients)	$6,000
Online Course	$3,000
Membership Site	$2,500
Total	$17,500

💡 **Authors who build multiple income streams create financial freedom.**

Next Steps: Your Success Blueprint

Immediate Actions

- ✅ **Schedule a strategy call** with **SayThat Publishing**
- ✅ **Start pre-launch marketing** (social media breadcrumbs)
- ✅ **Plan your speaking & consulting offers**

90-Day Goals

- ✅ **Complete manuscript & secure testimonials**
- ✅ **Book 2 speaking engagements**
- ✅ **Develop a coaching or consulting package**

One-Year Vision

- ✅ **Achieve bestseller status**
- ✅ **Book regular speaking engagements**
- ✅ **Launch digital products & corporate offers**

🚀 **The path to success is proven.** The only question is—will you take action?

Final Thoughts: From Author to Authority

Your book is **more than just words on paper**—it's the key to **unlocking multiple income streams, increasing your impact, and building long-term success.**

- 📌 **Write with purpose.**
- 📌 **Publish strategically.**
- 📌 **Market effectively.**
- 📌 **Scale systematically.**

If you're ready to **turn your book into a thriving business**, **Janelle Villiers Partnerships (JVP)** and **SayThat Publishing** are here to help.

📧 **Schedule your strategy call today by emailing:** janelle@jvillierspartnerships.com.

Let's build your author empire. 🚀

70

Conclusion: Your Journey Begins Now

You now have the blueprint to transform your **expertise, passion, and message** into a **bestselling book and thriving business.**

The only thing left? **Taking action.**

The Path Forward

Success doesn't happen by chance—it happens by **commitment, strategy, and execution.**

Let's recap the key elements of your journey:

- 📖 **Writing:** 30 minutes a day builds momentum.
- 🚀 **Publishing:** Strategic choices maximize impact.
- 📣 **Marketing:** Proven bestseller strategies work.
- 💰 **Income:** Multiple revenue streams await.
- 🌍 **Impact:** Your message can change lives.

Every successful author started **exactly where you are right now.** The difference? **They took the next step.**

Choose Your Path to Success

Wherever you are in your author journey, there's a **support system and strategy** to help you move forward.

📌 JVP Writing Support Programs

✅ The Author's Journey ($49/month)
- Monthly community meetings
- Exclusive access to recordings & resources

✅ The Author's Voyage ($4,000)
- 12-week structured program
- Weekly coaching & group sessions
- Personalized guidance

📣 *"I completed my entire manuscript in just two and a half months... I can't recommend The Author's Voyage enough!"* – Jacqueline Crider

✅ The Author Pioneer ($7,500)
- 16-week premium program
- Weekly **1-on-1 coaching**
- Deep editing & publishing guidance

💡 **Flexible Payment Options Available:**
✔ Monthly payment plans
✔ Sponsorship programs
✔ Custom schedules

📌 Publishing & Marketing Services

At **SayThat Publishing,** we provide:

✅ **A Dual-Editor System** – Get both **content editing and grammar editing** for the price of one.
✅ **Proven Bestseller Strategy** – We've helped authors hit **#1 on launch day.**
✅ **Boutique Quality Services** – You're not alone from **pre-launch to launch.**

📣 *"They're going to elevate your writing to a level you never thought possible and make your manuscript stand out in ways you never even imagined."* – Michael Takyi

📩 **Take action today:** Schedule your strategy call to discuss program options and payment plans that fit your needs.

Why Now Matters

Think about the books that changed your life.

Those authors faced the same doubts you might be feeling right now. The only difference? **They took action.**

📌 **Average author:** 5 years from idea to publication.
📌 **JVP & SayThat Publishing authors:** 6-12 months to bestseller status.

🚀 The **faster you take action, the faster your book impacts lives.**

Your Next Steps

📅 **This Week:**

✅ **Schedule your strategy call** with **JVP & SayThat Publishing**
✅ **Download your outline template** and get started
✅ **Begin your social media breadcrumbing** (pre-marketing)

📅 **This Month:**

✅ **Complete your book outline**
✅ **Set your official launch date**
✅ **Plan your revenue streams** (speaking, consulting, digital products)

📅 **This Quarter:**

✅ **Finish your manuscript**
✅ **Build your author platform** (website, social media, audience)
✅ **Prepare for your bestseller launch**

🚀 **Every small step brings you closer to success.**

The Investment Question

Before you decide whether to move forward, ask yourself:

📌 **Time Spent:** How long have you been thinking about writing a book?
📌 **Cost of Waiting:** What's the financial and personal cost of hesitation?
📌 **The Value of Your Message:** How many lives could your book impact?
📌 **Return on Investment:** Our authors **average 10-20x ROI** from speaking, coaching, and book sales.

📣 **Your book isn't just an idea—it's an opportunity.**

Final Thoughts: Your Book Is Your Legacy

Your book isn't just a dream—it's a **gateway to:**

🏆 **Professional Authority** – Position yourself as an expert in your field.
💰 **Multiple Income Streams** – Speaking, consulting, digital products, and more.
🌐 **Global Impact** – Your message has the power to change lives.
📖 **Personal Legacy** – A lasting contribution to the world.

At **JVP & SayThat Publishing**, we've helped countless authors **turn their expertise into bestselling books and thriving businesses.**

Now it's your turn.

📩 **Ready to begin?** Contact **JVP & SayThat Publishing** at janelle@jvilli erspartnerships.com today for your **personalized strategy session.**

🚀 **Let's make your book the foundation of your empire.**

<u>Appendix A: SayThat Publishing pricing</u>

PACKAGES FOR
EDITING &
PUBLISHING

PLATINUM PACKAGE*

- Author Community
- ISBN + Copyright
- Editing + Formatting
- Publishing to KDP & IS
- Cover design
- Beta Readers & Feedback
- Maintain email campaigns
- Amazon Bestseller optimization
- 20 podcast leads (guaranteed 1 podcast interview)

$3199

WRITE
EDIT
PUBLISH

GOLD PACKAGE*

- Author Community
- ISBN + Copyright
- Editing + Formatting
- Publishing to KDP & IS
- Cover design
- Beta Readers & Feedback

$1849

SILVER PACKAGE*

- Author Community
- Editing + Formatting
- Publishing to KDP & IS

$999

Editing
PRICING

EDITING PER WORD

- 0-10,000 words - flat fee: $250
- 10,000 - 30,000 words: $0.03/word
- 30,001 - 50,000 words: $0.018/word
- 50,001+ words: $0.0175/word

EXAMPLES

- 30,000 words (approx 60-70 pages) = $600
- 45,000 words (approx 90-100 pages) = $800
- 80,000 words (approx 160-170 pages) = $1400

- 50,000 words = $900
- 60,000 words = $1050
- 65,000 words = $1137.50
- 70,000 words = $1250
- 80,000 words = $1400
- 90,000 words (approx 245-255 pages) = $1,575
- 100,000 words (approx 260-270 pages) = $1,750

A La Carte PRICING

PUBLISHING TO KDP & IS

- $350 Flat fee up to 3 revisions
- $65 for every revision after the 3rd

ILLUSTRATED BOOK PUBLISHING TO KDP & IS

- $450 Flat fee up to 3 revisions
- $70 for every revision after the 3rd

ISBN + COPYRIGHT

- $400 Flat fee

BEST SELLER OPTIMIZATION

- $250 Flat fee

Appendix B: JVP Writing Worksheets

Follow this Blueprint to ensure your book's key messages resonate powerfully with readers.

My Book Blueprint

Book Title:

Every once in a while come back to your blueprint and make sure all of your key points (lessons) are in your book. If you want to add a major point, you can always add it! If you decide later to remove one, you can remove it! This outline is not set in stone but rather something that you can return to, to make sure you are on track and not forgetting any important point or any person important to the stories that illustrate your points.

What are 5 key points you want the readers to come away with:	1. _____ 2. _____ 3. _____ 4. _____ 5. _____
Of the 5 what are the top 3 key points:	1. _____ 2. _____ 3. _____
What is the #1 key point:	1. _____

Story Details

1. _____   1. _____
2. _____   2. _____
3. _____   3. _____
4. _____   4. _____
5. _____   5. _____

What is the chronological order in which they happen (in your life, or in the main character's life)?

a) _____ f) _____

b) _____ g) _____

c) _____ h) _____

d) _____ I) _____

e) _____ j) _____

Who are the people (characters) who helped play a MAJOR role during self-discovery and/or the journey?

1. _____

2. _____

3. _____

4. _____

5. _____

6. _____

How do these individuals fit the stories I will be sharing?

_____

_____

_____

_____

_____

_____

Start writing about one of the stories you described. You don't have to start at the beginning. You don't have to write it in chronological order at all. You can **edit** it into chronological order later. 😉

HAVE FUN!

Having Writer's Block? Try Roll-A-Story to get the creative inspiration going again!

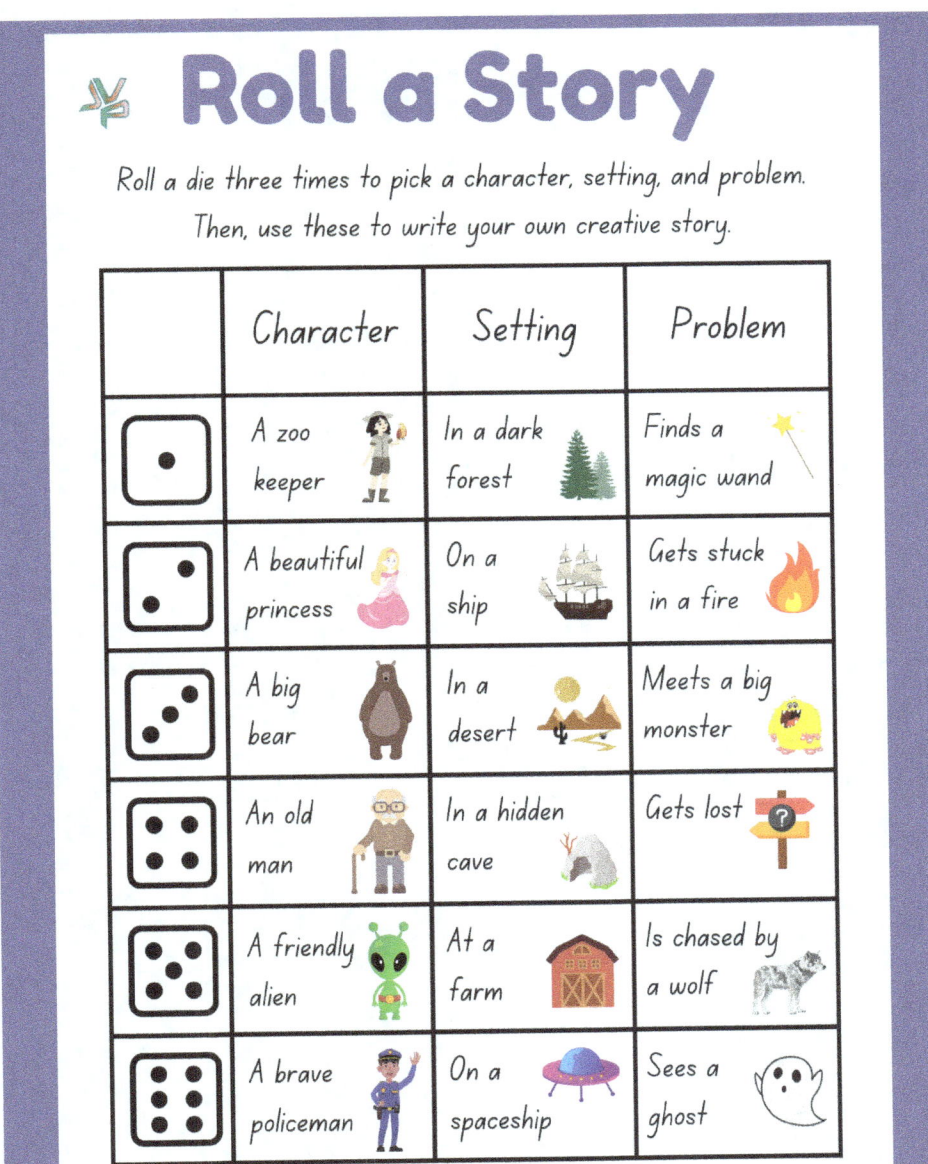

Roll a Story

Roll a die three times to pick a character, setting, and problem.
Then, use these to write your own creative story.

	Character	Setting	Problem
⚀	A zoo keeper	In a dark forest	Finds a magic wand
⚁	A beautiful princess	On a ship	Gets stuck in a fire
⚂	A big bear	In a desert	Meets a big monster
⚃	An old man	In a hidden cave	Gets lost
⚄	A friendly alien	At a farm	Is chased by a wolf
⚅	A brave policeman	On a spaceship	Sees a ghost

Acknowledgments

My deepest gratitude to God for bestowing upon me a calling that exceeds my wildest imagination and for planting the seed of this book in my heart.

To my parents: Your unwavering belief in my dreams has been my foundation. My love for you stretches beyond the stars.

This journey would have been impossible without Winston Broderick, my co-founder, business partner, and editor. Your visionary perspective, thought-provoking conversations, and remarkable patience with my scattered thoughts have been invaluable.

Derron Walker—my mentor and true ICON—your steadfast faith in my potential and strategic guidance have propelled me further than I ever thought possible.

I'm blessed by my inner circle of friends, family, and loved ones who hold me accountable in my professional endeavors yet provide sanctuary when I need to shed the "business persona." Your love sustains me. I love you.

Finally, my HEART OVERFLOWS with gratitude to each client who has become family. Unknowingly, you've furthered my mission of changing lives through books. Thank you for entrusting me with your literary treasures - your "babies." The privilege of nurturing your message and transforming your aspirations into reality has been one of my life's greatest honors.

With profound appreciation & gratitude,

Janelle

About the Author

Janelle Villiers is a bestselling author, publishing strategist, founder of Janelle Villiers Partnerships (JVP), and co-founder of SayThat Publishing. After transforming her own message into a bestselling book that opened doors to speaking engagements and coaching opportunities, she now helps others navigate the journey from concept to successful published author.

With her unique dual-editor approach and proven bestseller strategy, Janelle has guided numerous writers to #1 bestseller status while building sustainable businesses around their books. Through her coaching programs—Author's Journey, Author's Voyage, the Author Pioneer, and with SayThat Publishing services—she provides the accountability, structure, and expertise needed to turn writing dreams into published reality.

Connect with Janelle at www.janellevillierspartnerships.com

www.ingramcontent.com/pod-product-compliance
Lightning Source LLC
Chambersburg PA
CBHW080903120626
46555CB00008B/2936